DECLARATIONS
IN THE DESERT

LIFE-GIVING DECREES FOR THE DRY AND DUSTY VALLEYS OF LIFE

TARA SIERRA MOSELEY

Declarations in the Desert

Copyright © 2023 by Tara Sierra Moseley

Valley of Vision, LLC

All rights reserved.

Printed in the United States of America

ISBN Number: 979-8-218-11615-6

Unless otherwise indicated, all scripture quotations are taken from the
Amplified Version of the Bible. Public Domain.

Book Cover design and interior layout design by Tara Sierra Moseley

Cover Illustration by Silvia Ilona Klatt and Mackenna Cotten

Second paperback edition July 2023
in partnership with The Fedd Agency, Inc.

Declarations in the Desert is the first installment of *The Valley of Vision Trilogy*

For prints and other products, visit:
www.declarationsinthedesert.com

*May the Lamb receive
the reward of His suffering.*

"YOU WILL ALSO DECIDE AND DECREE A THING, AND IT WILL BE ESTABLISHED FOR YOU; AND THE LIGHT OF GOD'S FAVOR WILL SHINE UPON YOUR WAYS."
JOB 22:28

MAP THROUGH THE
DESERT

Valley of Health

Valley of Health Cont'd

Oasis of Living Water

Mountains of Life

Manna in the Wild

Manna in the Wild Cont'd

TO THE ONE DECLARING IN THE DESERT,

There are only two kingdoms, and every time we speak we are coming into alliance with one or the other.

Declarations are a powerful weapon given to us by God to legally crush the kingdom of darkness and to usher in the Kingdom of Light in our lives, families, cities, and nations.

Throughout time, a decree has been defined as an official order given by a legal authority. The act of declaring is agreeing with a particular statement that has been said or released.

To decree and declare is simply agreeing with the promises found in the Living Word and speaking them into your world. There is an assurance when you make a Godly decree or declaration - you are confident in both the source and the outcome. You believe and agree with the Truth of the scripture, you understand your legal authority as a child of the Most High God, and you speak with a confidence that God really is who He says He is.

authority *Remember who you are, your birthright as a son or daughter of Yahweh. There is no striving or relying upon the works of your hand. Simply pick up your sling and stone and declare with authoritative joy that which He has promised in His Word to His children.*

freedom *The visual layout of this book is important. It is a divine design merged with living words. The pages and sentence structure speak to the heart and move the spirit. It tends to defy the logic of grammar and standard sentence structure, allowing you to experience the areas of emphasis from the Holy Spirit. As you catch the cadence of the decree, you catch the fresh breath of Spirit and Truth. The empty spaces on the pages leave room for the manifestation of the promise: that where the Spirit of the Lord is, there is freedom. There is a holy freedom living in these pages and you will organically experience it- just as it is being declared from the Throne Room itself.*

declare *As you decree the Living Word over your life and the situations before you, you will see atmospheres begin to shift. The promises of God will begin to blossom in what was once the driest, dustiest parts of your life. These decrees are not just for you, but for the generations of lives to come. Entire family lines will experience the Promises of God because of the arrows of light that leave your mouth to extinguish the darkness of the enemy. Let not the dust of the desert keep you from the oasis of freedom that Jesus paid for with His body and blood.*

VALLEY OF
HEALTH

God's will is to heal.
As in Heaven as it is on Earth. There is no
sickness in Heaven. All sickness, disease, and
suffering is from the pit of Hell.
Declare His will to heal you.
Declaring in the midst of a valley of a health
crisis can shift the entire
atmosphere, ushering in winds of peace,
healing, and restoration. It is speaking out what
you are believing to happen,
regardless of what the terrain before you looks
like. The valleys of health may
appear ever winding, but these decrees will go
before you - through the
impassable, harsh, and dry deserts -
leading you into encounters with the
Father and into the land of promise.

He is Jehovah Rapha.

Decree with power.
Declare with authority.
Decree with confidence.

DECLARATION OF GOD'S WILL TO HEAL

I declare it is my Father's will to heal.

I release the declarative prayer of Jesus:

"Your kingdom come, your will be done, on Earth as it is in Heaven."

I declare there is no sickness, no disease, no suffering in Heaven,
and I stand in agreement with
your kingdom of divine health and your will of healing to be released upon this Earth.

I decree all sickness, all suffering, all infirmity is the work of Satan -
and the will of my Father is to heal and for me to walk in life and life abundant.

I declare through the wounds and stripes of Jesus, I am healed.
I declare through the bruises and beatings of Jesus, I am healed.
I declare through the chastisement and slander of Jesus, I am healed.

I declare nothing is impossible, no situation beyond saving -
And I call upon the nature of your name:
Jehovah Rapha, for you are the Lord who heals me!

MATTHEW 6:9-13, ISAIAH 53:4-5, EXODUS 15:26

DECREE OF HOPE

I declare a holy spark,
Lit by the fiery breath of the Almighty One,
To relight this wildfire of hope
That is kindled within me.

I declare this fire of Hope is fueled
By the plans, the thoughts, and holy majesty of my Lord!

I decree every damp, soaking
Branch of hope deferred
That has tried to suffocate this holy fire of hope within me -
Be incinerated now in the name of Jesus!

I declare a burning up of every spirit of despair,
Every spirit of sorrow, unhappiness, gloominess,
Every spirit of demonic pessimism, be set ablaze now!
For our God, He is a holy, devouring fire!

I declare He is alive, moving,
He is the all consuming fire!
All hopeless mountains melt away like wax in a fireplace
When the Lord of all the Universe draws near.

I declare I have been given hope,
Hope that is sure, steadfast, and dependable.
I decree no evil plots against me
Can carry a more powerful verdict than my very
Destiny scroll of hope and a future
My Father has rolled out before me!

I declare this hope
Burns with wisdom,
Is sweet like honey,
And brings a future glorious hope for me,

I decree it is mine,
To light every step of my life,
Nothing can darken or destroy this hope!

I declare the eyes of my heart are open!
Enlightened, aware, and radiant with the
Hope to which He, the God of our Lord Jesus Christ,
The glorious Father has given me as my inheritance.

I declare my hope does not wait upon the world
But upon the Lord Yahweh!
My strength is renewed!
I declare I am running and I will not grow weary,
I will not tire, I declare that I soar on wings like eagles!

I decree hope arise!
Arise, Arise, Arise!
The lifeless parts of me be resurrected!

I declare this holy destiny call of hope
Is burning bright within me!
You are my refuge and my shield;
My hope finds its home in Your Word.

I declare the wick is lit,
The altar is burning,
And this wildfire of hope is mine.

Burn with power,
With glory,
With justice,
With peace,
And with hope within me.

*PROVERBS 24:14, EPHESIANS 1:18,
1 PETER 1:18, PSALM 97:5, ROMANS
5:5, MICAH 7:7, PSALM 130:5,
ISAIAH 40:31, PSALM 119:114,
1 CORINTHIANS 13:13,
JEREMIAH 29:11, HEBREWS 6:19,
HEBREWS 11:1, ROMANS 15:13,
PROVERBS 13:12*

DECREE OF REVIVAL AND LIFE

I declare the name of the living,
Miraculous power of God,
The author of life,
The restorer of all that is shattered,
The very one whose breath awakens

REVIVAL!

Restore us, O Lord God of Hosts!
Revive us, Yahweh!
I declare revival is my birthright
As a child of God!
Hope, joy, and peace are my portion.

I declare a posture of reverence,
A spirit of humility over myself
As I stand in awe of Your deeds.
I remember the memorial stones
The history of your faithful and unconditional love
Recorded in the Living Word and in the very book of my own life.

I bind the voice of the liar
And declare the blood of Jesus
Over every false accusation
Every attempt to steal, kill, and destroy my destiny.

I declare Your face shines brighter,
Your fame resounds louder,
Your glory burns fiercer!

I declare a revival of your Spirit In my life,
Just as You promised in 1 Peter 5:10!

Restore me, DEPRESSION GO!
Secure me, ANXIETY LEAVE!
Strengthen me, FEAR BE GONE!
Establish me, HOPELESSNESS GO!

I declare revive us again!
May your Spirit break forth in every home, every city, and every nation!

I declare to every dead, sleeping, dormant
Part of my soul and spirit, AWAKEN!
I declare the graves clothes are torn apart
And the garments of revival are draped upon me now!

I cry out just as Elijah did!
"LORD my God, let this child's life return to him!"

Revival to my soul, to my very DNA!
To every crushed, dry, and beaten down part of me!

I declare be revived!

"And the Lord heard the voice of Elijah - and the soul of the child came
into him again, and he revived!"

I declare Your fame above every other name, Yahweh!
I declare Your right hand will never fail.

I declare joyful songs will be sung again
In the hearts and the homes,
I declare a loud shout of victory will echo throughout the
Very ground upon which I stand.

Revive us.

*1 KINGS 17:21-22, PSALM 118:15, JOB 42:5, HABAKKUK 3:2, PSALM 80:19, PSALM
80:18, 1 PETER 5:10, PSALM 85:6, AMOS 9:14, 2 CHRONICLES 7:14, JAMES 4:8,
1 KINGS 18:21, EPHESIAN 5:14, JEREMIAH 30:17*

DECLARE HE IS HEALER

I declare you are the Lord who heals me!

No spirit of sickness,
No spirit of suffering,
No spirit of infirmity,
No spirit of torment
Can withstand the healing power of my God
Who triumphantly decrees over my life:

"I will restore you to health and heal your wounds!"

To every cell in my body,
He is healer,
Restorer,
Reviver,
His name is Jehovah Rapha
And when I call to Him in my distress -
He heals me!

JEREMIAH 30:17

DECLARE A SOUND MIND

I declare I have a Sound Mind,
Immune to the compromises of the world!

I declare I have stable thoughts,
Set on things above, and not below.

I declare I have a holy cognitive process,
Anchored to the discernment of the trusted Holy Spirit.

I declare I have a protected and purified imagination,
Free of the lies and counterfeits of the evil one.

I declare my body is a temple,
Power from on High swirls about me,
Consecrating every impression, idea and reflection.

I declare my intellect is under the Lordship of Jesus,
Constantly being renewed and transformed by His Revelatory Glory.

I declare my dreams are sanctified,
Guarded and protected by the Lord of Hosts from all menacing and
Tormenting spirits.

I declare God's will for my life is
Void of fear, cowardice, and timidity
For He has filled my spirit to overflow with
Power from on high and benevolent love.

I declare I trust my Creator,   *2 TIMOTHY 1:7, ISAIAH 26:3,*
My mind rests in a pasture of perfect peace   *ROMANS 12:2, COLOSSIANS 3:2,*
As He guides me in the ways of righteousness.   *PSALM 23*

Power, love, and a sound mind are my inheritance.

DECREE OVER CHRONIC SICKNESS

I declare God's will is for me to be healed: mind, body, and soul.

For every cycle of infirmity and sickness in my body
To be stopped in the name of Jesus.

I declare sickness is not my inheritance,
And I rebuke any hold of the enemy in my life
Through fear, anxiety, despair, or disappointment.

I declare I am healthy.
I declare I am healed.
I declare my children and my children's children will walk in divine health
and prosperity in their bodies and minds.

I declare the spirit of fatigue has no legal right to my life
And I apply the blood of the Lamb over every
Aching bone and exhausted cell in my body.

I decree every spirit of pain, fatigue, and despair
Must leave in the name of Jesus.

I speak to every familiar spirit disguised as an invisible symptom,
Be gone! I bind you by the word of Jesus Christ who says
By His wounds I have been healed.

I declare a Holy Spirit reset over my thoughts and peace over my mind.
I declare His nearness over my comings and my goings.
Peace is my inheritance.

I declare my body is not a house of chronic sickness
But a thriving house of health and healing.

2 KINGS 20:5

I declare I am alive and a
Wellspring of life.
The Lord hears my prayers,
The Lord sees my tears,
And I declare He will heal me.

8

DECLARATION
OVER SUFFERING

I declare He is mighty, yet merciful,
All-powerful, yet kind.
I declare My Father sees me in my suffering, in my agony,
And He bends down,
Stooping from the Heavens in kindness,
To bestow His mercy upon me:
Wrapping my aching bones in living love,
And lifting my fainting body with His merciful arms.

When I am in agony,
I declare He is strong.
When I am trembling,
I declare He is safety.
When I feel unseen,
I declare He sees me.
When I am suffering,
I declare He heals me.

PSALM 6:2

DECLARATION OF
LIFE OVER DEATH

I declare, today,
As Heaven and Earth are my witnesses,
I choose as an act of my own free will
Life and blessings,
And I say NO to every spirit of death and curses!

I decree life over death!
For the Word is near me -
Living in my heart,
Flowing from my mouth,
And I make a lifelong declaration
Of obedience unto the King:
The Giver of all life and all goodness!

YAHWEH!

I desire to walk in the paths of His ways,
Each and every day!
To guard, protect, and keep His commandments, statutes, and ordinances -
Not out of religious duty,
But out of holy adoration and reverential love.

My love for Him opens my ears to hear His voice,
And I am joined to Him, never to be separated,
Tethered to the Giver and Restorer of Life.

I declare I will live,
I declare I will increase,
I declare I will prosper,
And the blessings of Yahweh are alive,
Living within the land He is leading me to possess.

I choose life not death,
Blessings not curses,
And I decree my life is marked by the love of the Lord,
And joyful, laid down obedience to Him.

My life is His life!

I declare blessing, protection, and a life prolonged
Over my bloodline - every door of death and curses,
I slam shut now with the victorious, all-powerful
Blood of the Lamb!

I decree to every demonic spirit,
My Father, the Most High,
Who split the seas with a mighty blast of His nostrils,
Who rides on the wings of Spirit-Wind,
Whose brilliance bursts forth with lightning bolts and hail,
Who speaks with a thunder voice from the sky

That is my God and He is witness to my decree:

Life not death is my choice!
Blessings not curses are my choice!
May it be recorded now,

Hallelujah! Hallelujah! Hallelujah!

DEUTERONOMY 30:11-20

DECLARING DRY
BONES TO LIFE

I declare to the bones scattered in the valley,
The dead, the dry, the dusty,
Hear the word of the Lord!
Receive the breath from the four winds
And live!

I declare to the slain, the dead bones, live!

I declare what is dead, is now rattling with life!

What was broken is mending,
What was shattered is restored,
What was constricted is breathing
What was dead with dust is filling with the breath of life!

EZEKIEL 37:4-7

DECREE OF STRENGTH AND COURAGE

Just as David stood before Goliath and declared:
"Blessed be the Lord, My Rock - My Strength"
I declare there is only one
Strong, safe, and secure place for me.

It is in God alone who gives me strength.

I declare He is my shelter of love
And also my fortress of Faith,
He wraps himself around me as a secure shield.

I declare I am hidden
From my enemies and the deceiver.

I am hidden in the house of
My refuge
My deliverer
My helper
The only one who can subdue
The enemies before me.

I declare
Courage
Strength
Over myself now.

I declare My king
The only King
The God of the Angel Armies
Will not forsake or forget me.

I am loved and protected by the one
Who will never fail me.

PSALM 144:1-2,
DEUTERONOMY 31:6

DECLARATION OVER PANIC

I declare I am not alone.
Even in the darkest valleys, I will not be afraid.
I declare His comfort wraps around me,
Blanketing me in safety and assurance.

I declare a deep infilling of the spirit of Peace in my body,
Overcoming every spirit of panic and dread.

I declare my days were not made to be spent
In panic and worry,
And I declare breakthrough
Over every tormenting spirit sent against me.

I declare He knows me;
He will not leave me in
the swirls of the river or the flames of the fire.
I declare He is with me: rescuing, restoring, and renewing.

I declare I know He is God,
His plans are good,
His ways are kind,
I can rest inside of His Peace.

ISAIAH 43:1-2,
PSALM 23:4,
PSALM 46:10

DECREE OVER ANXIETY

I declare He is the God of Hope,
calming all anxiety with the blanket of His Peace.
I declare He is the God of compassion,
caring deeply for the tears and the dreams of my heart.

I declare the Devil is a liar,
and all spirits of anxiety and chaos are from the pit of Hell.

I declare Yahweh knit me together in my mother's womb,
and the plans for my life are overflowing with goodness,
with peace, with joy.

I declare unshakable peace,
all spirits of restlessness and worry no longer torment my life.
I declare rest,
all spirits of fatigue and exhaustion leave my body.
I declare a sound mind,
all spirits of distraction and scattered thoughts flee.
I declare patience,
all spirits of irritation and chaos depart.
I declare joy,
all spirits of despair and hopelessness are gone.
I declare deep restoration,
all spirits of trauma and sickness are rendered powerless.

I declare my trust lives in Him,
filling me with peace,
ridding me of all spirits of anxiety,
and overflowing my life with hope by the power of the Holy Spirit.

ROMANS 15:13, 1 PETER 5:6-7, JEREMIAH 29:11,
PSALM 9:9, ISAIAH 41:10, PSALM 34:18

DECLARATION
OF HEALING

I cry out to you Lord,
And I make a declaration to every sickness,
Every blocking spirit of infirmity,
And burden of trouble,
You are no more than a pebble in my path!
And my God,
YAHWEH,
Hurls you with His mighty,
Strong,
Righteous right hand
Out of my body,
Out my mind,
And out of my destiny!

For He has sent out His Word,
Healed me!
Saved me!
Rescued me!
And I decree I walk in victory,
Carrying the Spirit of the living testimony of Jesus Christ
In every cell and fiber of my being.

For you are wondrous, Lord,
And I declare I live to praise you.
In your name I fight my battles!

PSALM 107:19-21

DECLARATION OVER TRAUMA

I declare the past trauma inflicted upon me will not dictate the
future of my destiny.
I declare there are marvelous plans for my life.

I declare the Lord sees me in my mourning,
comforting me in my place of pain.

I declare the holy fire of God around my mind,
protecting me from any and all recurring and triggering
traumatic memories.

I declare my life is precious, valuable, and worthy -
I am seen and known by the Father of Life.
I declare the Lord cares for my sorrows,
not one tear falls without His notice.

PSALM 56:6,
MATTHEW 5:4-5,
2 CORINTHIANS 4:16,
PSALM 31:18

I declare His Spirit wraps around me,
pushing away every spirit of trauma, pain, and shame.

I declare hope, praise, and joy are the banners over my life.

DECREEING MY
VOICE HAS VALUE

I declare my voice has value,
Carrying the authority and the power
To take back what the enemy has stolen.

JOSHUA 6:16

DECLARATION
OVER DEATH

I declare I will live,
I declare I will not die,
I declare I am walking out of the valley of the Shadow of Death,
Declaring with my mouth, with my spirit, with my life
The goodness of the Lord as I run, dance, and reside in the land of the living.

PSALM 27:13

DECLARE REST OVER EXHAUSTION

I declare His presence is with me,
lifting me from the chains of chaos and anxiety
and gifting me with deep rest.

I declare a release from the toiling and the striving
as I follow the footsteps of His Spirit into His rest.

I declare I will rest in tender green pastures,
He will lead me beside the still and restful waters.

I declare that the Lord, the God of the Angel Armies,
refreshes and restores my life.

I declare a divine exchange,
my weariness, my burdens,
for His Rest, His Peace.

I declare rest and peace live within me as
I build a dwelling place in the shelter of the Most High.

I declare He is gentle and humble in heart,
and I rest within the hidden places of His presence, safe and protected.

I declare rest
in my soul,
in my spirit,
in my body,
for He is the Almighty One, and His yoke is easy and His burden is light.

I declare I will lie down in peace,
and I will rise in peace,
for the Lord, alone,
makes me dwell in safety.

PSALM 31;20, PSALM 91:1-2,
EXODUS 33:14, PSALM 4:8,
MATTHEW 11:28, MATTHEW 11:29

DECLARATION
OF BREATH

I declare the Spirit of God made me,
and the very breath of the Almighty gives me life.

I decree to all breathing-related attacks of the enemy:
be stopped now by the very Hand of God!

JOB 33:4,
Who created the heavens and stretched them out,   *GENESIS 2:7,*
Who spread out the earth and its offspring,   *ISAIAH 42:5*
Who gives breath to the people on it!

I declare I will breathe deeply,
inhaling and exhaling in peace,
shalom breath into my lungs.
I declare no weapon formed against my breath will prosper.

Breathe again.

DECLARATION OVER
LYME DISEASE

I declare my blood is cleansed,
free of bacteria, co-infections, mold, toxicity, and
alive with the miraculous power of Jesus.

I declare the diagnosis of Lyme is broken off my destiny,
and the destiny of John 10:10 abundant life is released over my life.

I declare a joyful heart beats in my chest,
supplying health,
vibrant life,
and toxin-free blood to my body.

I declare I am healed, restored,
and whole, in Jesus name.   *PROVERBS 17:22, ISAIAH 38:16, JOEL 3:21*

DECLARATION OVER THE FEAR OF MAN

I declare I will not be trapped by the snares of the fear of man,
I declare I am courageous,
Refusing to bow at the feet of men.

I declare the supreme authority in my life is Yahweh,
And I walk in joyful reverence to His commands.

I declare the Truth of the Word over the Lies of Culture!

I declare there is safety in the call of the King,
The applause of man is empty noise,
I declare I do not perform in the circus of men,
I declare I live for Yahweh, and Yahweh alone.

I declare I love the Lord,
With all my heart,
With all my soul,
And with all my mind.

*MATTHEW 22:37, ACTS 5:29,
PROVERBS 29:25,
DEUTERONOMY 1:17,
1 SAMUEL 15:24*

I declare I will not listen to the cackling of men
Over the voice of the King.
Fear must bow,
Intimidation must flee,
I declare my trust is in the Lord,
The pressures and slanders of men will not trap me.

I declare The Holy Spirit fills me with power from on High,
A shield of boldness and kingdom identity cover me,
Extinguishing every fiery arrow of fear sent by the Evil One.

I declare with Peter and the apostles:
"We must obey God rather than men."
I declare the voice of God reigns above all the whispers of the world.

DECLARATION OVER TUMORS AND CYSTS

I declare no weapon formed against my body will prosper,
All tumors, cysts, and fibroids in my body must shrink in The
Name of Jesus.
I declare Jesus is healer, restoring my body from all spirits of
Infirmity and sickness.

I declare gracious words of peace to my body,
Sweet to the soul,
And healing to my bones.

I declare my body is a temple of the Holy Spirit,
And release the fire of the Holy Spirit to consume all
Foreign growths attacking my body,
I declare shalom to my nervous system,
Calming any and all hormonal imbalances,
And blanketing all inflammation with
The cooling breath of Heaven.

ISAIAH 54:17,
PROVERBS 16:24,
1 CORINTHIANS 6:19-20,
PSALM 41:3

I declare to each and every cell in my body, be filled with
Life, peace, and health.

DECLARATION OF LIFE

I decree life,
Wake up dead things.
I decree arise,
Be resurrected.
I decree the power, the authority, and the living breath of Yahweh,
Into all that is dead, dormant, and asleep.
Awaken, in the name of Jesus.

EPHESIANS 5:14

DECLARATION OVER AUTOIMMUNE DISORDERS

I declare a breaking of any agreement with an autoimmune disorder diagnosis.
I decree a coming into agreement with the promise of abundant life
given to me by Jesus.

I declare life over my body,
all spirits of fatigue, exhaustion, achiness, and brain fog
must bow at the name of Jesus and leave my body now.

I declare my life will not be defined by flareups or managing symptoms,
I declare wholeness and freedom mark my days.

I declare my spirit of faith silences the spirit of inflammation,
canceling any right it has to operate in my body.

I declare restoration over my body, over my life;
the days the enemy stole through sickness will be returned.

I declare the spirit of depression and death attached to autoimmune
be canceled and removed;
I call my spirit back to life in the name of Jesus.

I declare healing and life over every symptomatic spirit of autoimmune.
I declare I will walk, run, and dance in the land of the living.

MARK 5:34

DECLARATION
IN THE WAITING

I declare I wait with eyes fixed upon the King:
filling me with patience in the waiting,
overwhelming me with strength in the contending,
blanketing me with comfort in the suffering,
and gifting me peace in the disconcerting.

I declare patience and peace in His Presence.

I declare His Presence washes away the residue of the waiting,
breathing the breath of life into the despairing and dying.

I declare my whole being awaits Him, is fixed on the King:
waiting, listening, and confident my God hears me.

I declare I do not live in my own understanding,
I make my refuge in the trustworthy House of the Lord.

I declare I wait for Him,
Feeding on the Word and resting in His Promises.   *MICAH 7:7,*
PSALM 130:5,
PROVERBS 3:5-6

DECLARATION OVER DEPRESSION

I declare a mighty outpouring of Peace over every spirit of depression
plaguing my body, attacking my mind, and suffocating my spirit.

I declare I am not alone and silence every lying spirit of isolation,
and I cry out Abba Father,
releasing my heavy burdens
and laying all depressing, anxious thoughts at His feet.

I declare He delights in giving me rest,
blanketing me in peace,
and pouring joy over every depressed and despairing part of my spirit.

I declare my thoughts are stable,
my mind is at ease and focused.

I declare I will sleep through the night,
my thoughts sanctified in truth and purity,
and my joy for life will return.

I declare AWAKEN to my heart,
to remember and be activated in the joyous destiny of my life:
hope, prosperity, and a future.

I declare my life is not an accident or mistake,
I was created and purposed for this very time on the Earth.

I declare I will walk through this valley of depression triumphantly,
and I will laugh, dance, and be overwhelmed with joy again.

I declare I will live and not die.
this time of depression is not the Truth declared over my future.

2 CORINTHIANS 7:6,
2 PHILIPPIANS 4:8, JOHN 16:33,
JEREMIAH 29:11, MATTHEW 11:28,
PSALM 23:4, DEUTERONOMY 31:8

DECLARATION OVER PARKINSON'S

I cry out to you, Lord,
And I make a declaration to every afflicting spirit of Parkinson's,
You are no more than a pebble in my path!
And my God,
YAHWEH,
Hurls you with His mighty,
Strong,
Righteous right hand
Out of my body,
Out my mind,
And out of my destiny!

I declare stability over every tremor,
Peace over every tremble.
I declare wholeness in my body
From the top of my head to the soles of my feet.

For He has sent out His Word,
Healed me!
Saved me!
Rescued me!
And I decree I walk in victory,
Carrying the Spirit of the living testimony of Jesus Christ
That is alive in every cell and fiber of my being.

You are wondrous, Lord,
And I declare I live to praise You.

PSALM 107:19-21

DECLARATION OVER BLOOD DISORDERS

I declare the blood of Jesus is the most powerful substance in the universe.
I release the healing, purifying power of the blood of Jesus over myself.

I declare my blood is cleansed!

I declare the healing touch of Jehovah Rapha to every blood cell in my body,
Be healed now,
Be whole now,
Be regulated now.

I declare He heals all my diseases.
I rebuke every spirit of sickness sent against my blood cells.
I declare healing paid for by the blood of the Lamb.

PSALM 34:18, PSALM 103:3

DECREE OVER BEING FORGOTTEN

I declare I am not,
Never will be,
And cannot be forgotten.

Yahweh himself
Proudly calls me His own.
He delights in the intricacies of my being
And the adventures within my heart.

I declare I am known.
Even if abandoned by my own,
My Heavenly Father never leaves,
His love always finds me.

I declare the lies of isolation and despair
Will never be louder than the
Shouts of unconditional love and adoption
By the One who marked me as fearfully
And wonderfully made.

I declare my worth is not determined by those around me,
But by the One who knows me.

I declare Your strong right hand
Safely holds me.
Loneliness is not my destiny.

I declare I am not forgotten.
And I never will be.

PSALM 23:4, MATTHEW 28:20, PSALM 27:10

DECLARATION OVER NIGHT TERRORS

I declare I do not have a spirit of fear,
and I break agreement with every spirit of fear that has
come to awaken and torment me in the night.

I declare I am safe,
living in the Shelter of the Most High.
I declare I can rest,
relaxing in the Shadow of the Almighty.
I declare I can sleep,
peacefully lying in the safe Refuge of my God.

I declare my night terrors end now -
no fear, no anxiety, no sudden wakings in the dark will
come near me,
for He has assigned His angels to protect, guard,
and care for me.

I declare I trust Him and His Word!

I declare as I lie down, I dream the dreams of God,
for my mind is seated in heavenly places.
I declare I am strong, courageous, and protected by the
God of the Angel Armies.

I declare I rest peacefully, my spirit is calm,
comforted, and refreshed.
I declare I am never alone -
I am always protected by my Father.

PSALM 4:8, PSALM 91:1-2

DECLARATION OVER EYES

I declare healing over my eyes,
By the stripes of Jesus,
All sinister attacks of the enemy must stop.

I declare the healing power of the
Compassion of Jesus over my eyes,
Healthy eyes to gaze upon His creation,
Fresh eyes to see His Glory.
Clear eyes to carry out my destiny.

I declare a removal of the manifestation of fear
Over my eyes,
I will not worry or be filled
With anxious thoughts,
I declare a holy reversal upon any plans of the
Enemy to torment my eyes!

I declare a touch of the hand of Jesus
Upon my Eyes:
Eyes opening,
Infirmity leaving,
Peace returning.

I declare healing is mine,
He is Jehovah Rapha,
I will not waiver,
For He who promised is faithful.

HEBREWS 10:23, MATTHEW 9:27-30, JOHN 9:6-7

DECLARATION OVER CANCER

I declare I will live and not die!
I declare cancer is defeated by the stripes on my Savior's back!
I declare no sickness, no suffering, no form of cancer
will keep me from fulfilling the joyous destiny scroll of my life!

I break any agreement with a spirit of death spoken over me,
and I declare the living, resurrecting name of Yeshua over my life.
With the authority gifted to me by Jesus,
I speak to every malignant cell in my body
and command you to shrink and dissipate now.

I declare the destiny over my life is
to walk, to run, to dance, to sing, to laugh
in the fullness of life that Jesus paid for with
His body and blood on the cross!

I declare cancer will not steal the joy of my day or the minutes of my life,
for joy and a full life are gifted to me through the victory of Jesus Christ.

I rebuke every demonic spirit of cancer, foreign growth,
tumors, and every sick cell -
I declare life, restoration, and a desire to live over my DNA.

I break every curse of infirmity, cancer, and sickness sent against my life!

I declare joy over depression!
I declare courage over fear!
I declare peace over anxiety!
I declare hope over despair!

I declare restoration to all that has been stolen!
I declare life over my soul.
I declare I will live and not die.

ISAIAH 38:16

DECLARATION OVER A DIAGNOSIS

I declare no weapon formed against me will prosper!
I decree an agreement with my destiny scroll of life,
written before I ever took a breath on this Earth!

I decree the words of my Savior over my life:
"I came that they may have life, and have it in abundance,"
and I decree a breaking of any legal agreement with words of death or
destruction in the form of a medical diagnosis that has been released over me!

I declare I listen to One voice,
the only voice,
the One who breathed the breath of life into my body,
and I declare I am a child of the King,
and the blood of Jesus speaks a victorious word over my life!

I declare my feet are planted on solid rock,
The Rock that is higher than I,
and no anxiety, fear, or despair will enter my spirit or soul.

I declare I believe!
I believe healing power flows from Yeshua,
Healing all!
Every infirmity! Every sickness! Every ailment!
Every mental and physical affliction!

I declare His will is to heal and I stand in agreement with His will:
On Earth as it is in Heaven
and I receive the healing that was purchased on the cross with
His body and with His blood!

I declare the powerful yet peaceful voice of the Comforter speaks louder
and holds more value than any whisperings of science or medical diagnoses.

I silence the voice of the destroyer,
I rip out every spirit of fear,
and I declare I believe in the miraculous power from on High!

I declare by the stripes on Yeshua's back
every sickness, infirmity, and suffering was eradicated.

I declare I follow close to Him, His right hand holding on to me.
I declare under His wings, I rest.

I declare by His stripes,
the wounds upon His body,
His blood poured out,
I am healed.

I declare
Jehovah Rapha
over every spirit of sickness sent against my life!

LUKE 6:19,
MATTHEW 4:23, MATTHEW 9:35,
MATTHEW 14:14, MATTHEW 10:1

DECLARATION OVER FEAR AND CONFUSION

I declare I am created in the image of my Father,
and in Him:
there is no fear,
there is no confusion,
there is no cowardice.

I decree fear was not given to me by my Father,
and I declare the words spoken over me by
the One who breathed the breath of life into me:

"You did not receive a spirit of slavery that returns you to fear,
but you received the Spirit of sonship"

And as a child of the Kingdom,
I declare peace is my portion,
Sonship is my birthright,
and I tear down every suffocating, hiding, lying spirit of fear
and confusion in my life.

I declare fear, you are dethroned,
confusion, you are destroyed and eradicated
by the King of Kings, the Lord of Lords,
Jesus Christ, who came willingly and said:

"I am leaving you with a gift—peace of mind and heart.
And the peace I give is a gift the world cannot give.
So don't be troubled or afraid."

I declare I am not afraid, I am not troubled!

I decree a demarcation line,
right now,
in the spirit and the natural,
against every spirit of fear and confusion that has been sent
to entrap my mind,
enslave my body,
control my health,
and delay my destiny.

I speak the blood of Jesus against you - be bound now - in the name of Yeshua.

I declare an agreement with the promise of my Savior,
peace of mind,
peace of heart,
is mine because I am His.

I declare I have been given power,
love, and a sound mind.

ROMANS 8:15, JOHN 14:27, II TIMOTHY 1:7, JOHN 12:15

DECREE OVER DESPAIR AND DISAPOINTMENT

I decree a release of the life of Yahweh, flooding every dark and dim place in my spirit with the light of Christ, driving out every spirit of disappointment and despair!

I declare a strengthening of my inner being by the promises of His Word - stirring within me His faith, His hope, and His courage.

To every spirit of disappointment wrapping itself in despair and hopelessness, I speak to you now with the authority of the Lord who is with me like a mighty warrior:

You will not prevail in my life!
I declare an uprooting of every seed planted from a moment of disappointment and a cutting down of every tree grown in a season of despair in my life and in my blood line.

I decree a waterfall of living glory from the throne room of the Most High, washing away all hurt, all disappointment, all despair.

I declare He cares for me
And the concerns of my heart I lay before Him,
For my hopes and my dreams safely live within the hands of Yahweh.

I declare I will not be rattled by the winds of disappointment or the storms of despair; He is the solid, immovable rock upon which I build my life.

I declare I am a lover of God, sitting beside Him,
with a joyful feast of gladness set before us -
despair and disappointment have no place at our table!

I decree to my spirit man,
Rest,
His ways are perfect.
Peace,   *PROVERBS 10:28, PROVERBS 11:23, PSALM 119:116,*
His plans are flawless.   *JEREMIAH 20:11, PSALM 9;18, JOHN 1:3-5*
Hope,
He is forever faithful.

DECLARING HIS
DAILY HEALING

I declare peace,
Continual healing,
And daily freedom are mine,
Springing forth from my fountain of faith in my Lord, Yahweh.

MARK 5:34

DECREE OVER GRIEF

I declare light in the darkness,
a glowing radiance of the lamp of the Lord,
flooding all spirits of
grief, mourning, and sadness
in my heart,
in my mind,
and in my body.

I declare to my spirit:
receive the Comforter who brings,
light to darkness,
joy to mourning,
comfort to grief.

I declare He is near me,
listening and tending to my tears,
wrapping His healing arms around
the aching, shattered and broken
parts of my heart.

I declare He is the one saves my crushed spirit,
breathing the breath of light and life
into the dark and dying,
lifting off spirits of grief.

I declare He is my breakthrough,
and I will dance, again!
His confident right hand removes the
heaviness of mourning and wraps me
in the glory garments of praise.

I declare joy will come in the morning,
He is my lamp turning darkness into light.

ROMANS 8:28, PSALM 34:18, PSALM 30:11,
REVELATION 21:4

DECREE OVER INFERTILITY

I declare I am not alone.
I walk in ever-increasing health
By the body and the blood of Jesus.

I declare I am fruitful.
My husband is fruitful.
Our bodies are whole and strong.

I declare I am purposed to carry and nurture life.
My womb is whole and my body fertile.

I declare I am worthy,
My steps covered in Grace.
I declare I belong,
Every spirit of isolation has no place in my life.

I declare a blessing over my doctors
But I do not partner with any
Negative words, diagnoses, or medical reports
Spoken over my body and my family line.

I declare He is the giver of Life,
My life is marked by
Fruitfulness,
Health in all areas,
And Kingdom favor.

I declare I live under supernatural protection
I am never alone
Every tear, He catches.
Surrounded by angels on assignment
My prayers are powerful.
I am marked by Heaven for a legacy of life.

In the name of Jesus,
I declare
Fear, leave now.
Stress, be gone.
Worry, you have no home here.
Anxiety, I uproot you.
Hopelessness, get out now.
Medical diagnosis, you are not the truth declared over my life.
Every attack of the enemy,
I break you in the name of Jesus.

I declare over my
Body, be still.
Know He is God.
Mind, be filled with the
Everlasting Peace of Jesus.
Soul, rest.
Heart, be lightened.
Womb, you are fruitful.

I declare I walk in divine health.
I am fertile.
I am whole.
I am outrageously loved.

I declare with God, all things are possible.
I will not be overwhelmed.
Nothing will shake me.
I am worthy.
I am loved.
I am not forgotten.
I declare I am never alone.

LUKE 1:37, ACTS 3:16, DEUTERONOMY 8;2,
GENESIS 1:28, 1 SAMUEL 2:21

DECREE OF PEACE

I declare to every spirit of anxiety, chaos, and restlessness:

PEACE, BE STILL.

PEACE, BE STILL.

PEACE, BE STILL.

I declare trouble will not plague my spirit,
I declare fear will not attack my mind,
I declare anxiety will not possess my thoughts,
for my mind is steadfast on Yahweh,
keeping me in perfect, unshakable peace.

I decree the peace of this world is
fleeting, counterfeit, and false,
and I break any agreement with it!

I declare the living words of Yeshua:
'Peace I leave with you; my peace I give to you.
Not as the world gives do I give to you.'

I receive this peace and make a decree over the days of my life:

I declare prayer is my weapon and
thankfulness my armor,
I come confidently before Yahweh,
and step into an outpouring of His Peace
that surpasses all earthly understanding!

I declare the Prince of Peace is with me all my days,
gifting me with Shalom Peace:
originating from the only true source,
the hand of the Lord,
the righteous, sovereign, and saving King
who will swallow up death forever and wipe away every tear!

I declare peace himself is with me,
gifting me peace at all times and in every way.

2 THESSALONIANS 3:16, ISAIAH 26:3, ISAIAH 25:10, ISAIAH 25:9, REVELATION 21:4,
JOHN 14:27, PHILIPPIANS 4:6-7, MATTHEW 5:9, PSALM 29:11, 1 CORINTHIANS 14:33

DECREE OVER SHAME

I declare the residue of shame in my life
Is washed away by the blood of Jesus.

I declare His yoke is easy
And His burden is light,
I will not
And I do not
Carry any shame, disgrace, or humiliation.

I declare my past does not define my future,
For I am a born-again citizen of the Kingdom of Heaven,
A child of the Most High.
And I wear the garments of honor
Placed upon my shoulders by
The King of Justice, the King of Righteousness,
My loving Heavenly Father.

I decree I refuse to carry the weight of any past decisions or situations; my past
does not disqualify me for my future.

Just as Mary Magdalene was the first one to see the resurrected Christ,
I declare I am also worthy to walk with worth, free of shame and guilt.
I declare there is no condemnation in Christ.

I declare my face is like flint,
Disgrace and shame hold no power over me,
For the Lord, my God decrees "worthy" over me.

ISAIAH 54:4, ISAIAH 50:7, 1 JOHN 1:9

DECLARATION TO FEEL AGAIN

I declare the numbness is leaving,
The heart of stone is turning to a heart of flesh.

I declare pour out the Oil of Joy,
Wash away my tears.
I live to swim in the glorious mysteries of His Living Spirit.

I declare I will laugh again,
I declare I will be moved to joyful tears again,
I declare I will sing again.

Wake up sleeping heart,
Feel again.
Wake up slumbering lungs,
Breathe again.
Wake up tired shoulders,
Be upright again.

I declare the life of God into the deepest valleys of my soul,
Be revived in the name of Jesus.

PSALM 126:5-6

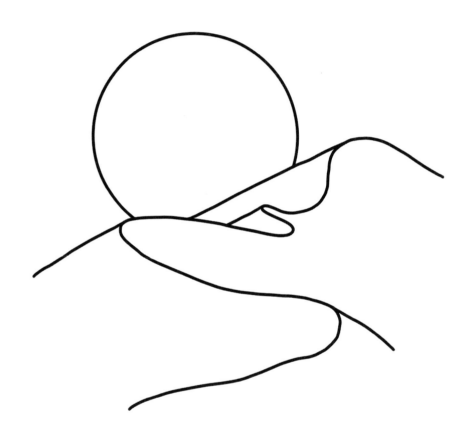

OASIS OF
LIVING
WATER

The winds of God are howling. Blowing through the caves, sweeping through the mountains and the valleys - catching the pages of destiny scrolls written long before breaths were ever taken.

As you declare and decree His name into the swirling mirages of the desert, you will find oases of living water to drink from. You will find rest under His shadow and peace in His Spirit. He is the caretaker and the provider. Trust Him.

He is Jehovah Jireh.

DECLARATION OF AN OASIS

I declare an oasis in my life,
for Yeshua has spoken to the thirsty dusty lands of my heart,
and an oasis of life is arising.

I declare pools of living water,
ripples of refreshment and replenishment,
flood the cracked and dead,
washing away the barren and dry.

I declare Resurrection life swirls in the wellsprings of my heart,
what was dead and gone is living and thriving,
for Yeshua,
the Author of Life,
has spoken,
and an oasis is arising.

PSALM 107:35

DECREE OF LIVING WATER

I decree a release of living waters,
a drying up of the counterfeit streams,
and a release of rushing living waters in my life!

I shut off every false and tainted water source in my generational line!
I declare an infilling from the only source -
the well of water springing up unto eternal life in Yeshua!

My trust is in Him and
my innermost being marked by Him
with rushing, flowing, living waters
from which I will never thirst again!

I decree this promise from Yeshua over my life:
"Whoever drinks of the water that I will give him shall never thirst!"

To my dry, dusty valley seasons,
be restored by the rivers of living water!
To my parched throat,
be refreshed with the living water!
To my dried out dreams,
be saturated in living water!

I declare to the brackish, stagnant puddles in my life,
be overcome now with a torrential, cascading waterfall of living water.

Renewal!
Restoration!
Refreshment!
Replenishment!

I declare the mighty waters of Yeshua to drench my spirit now!

I decree His rushing waters to wash over every home, every city, every state!

I declare this nation is a nation drinking from the fount of eternity,
Jesus!

I declare I have a fountain of living water leaping up,
bubbling up within me,
I am alive with the Spirit of God.

I thirst no more!

*JOHN 4:14, JOHN
7:38*

DECLARATION
OF VINDICATION

I declare sitting in the quiet with You
unlocks freedom for me.

As I commune with You
in the quiet,
I humbly renounce all
filth, all dirt, all defilement.

I declare my spirit receives Your Word:
Implanted,
Rooted,
Alive,
Thriving,
Within my heart.

I declare the Word has the power
to vindicate and rescue my soul.

JAMES 1:21

DECREE OF WILDFIRE

I declare a wildfire of Your love
To burn across my life,
Consuming anything that
is not of You.

I declare I am a lover
of Your Word,
Your promises glow
With a refining wildfire
That rages within me.

PSALM 97:3,
PSALM 119:140

DECREE OF SPIRIT AND TRUTH

I decree Spirit!
I decree Truth!

The hour is here,
When the true worshippers
RISE UP in Reverence and FALL DOWN in Adoration -
Humbling themselves in homage before the Almighty One.

I declare He is God!
Spirit, Breath, and Wind - the Father of All.
No mountain can contain the worship His name deserves.

I decree into the East, into the West, into the North, into the South,
Worship the Lord in Spirit and Truth!

I declare I am a child of Yahweh,
Born from above,
Dancing in Spirit and Truth,
Walking with His Wisdom,
Breathing the breath of His Freedom.

I declare my heart beats with purity,
A burning desire to know Him,
In Spirit and in Truth,
To worship Him,
In Spirit and in Truth,
To make His name known above all the swirls of the world.

I declare my worship is not unto platform or applause.
For the Spirit of Truth lives within me,
Teaching, leading and guiding me into the
Whole Truth.

I declare all Scripture is breathed out by God,
The Alpha, the Omega, the beginning and the end!

I declare honor unto the Holy Spirit!
I trust His voice.
I declare I am a beloved student of Truth, my ears are open -
For when He speaks, I listen.
For when He declares things that are coming, I listen.

I declare I am a worshiper,
A laid-down lover,
A reveler in the mysteries,
A follower of The Way,
I declare God is Spirit -
And those who worship Him
MUST
Worship in Spirit and Truth!

JOHN 4:24, JOHN 16:13, 2 CORINTHIANS 3:17

DECLARATION OF MY FIRST LOVE

I declare He is my first love,
The One who loved me first,
Before I ever took a breath on this Earth,
He set me apart.

I declare He is Lord Jehovah,
The all-consuming fire,
I declare my goodness is
From Your very presence!

I declare there is no greater love than this:
To lay down one's life for one's friends.
He loved me first
And sent His Son,
As the atoning sacrifice for my sins.

I declare His love
Comes before all this world can offer.
I long for Him
For apart from Him
There is no good thing.

I declare a tearing down of any idols
Or any counterfeit I have put before Him.

I declare my soul's desire is Him,
Hear my footsteps as I come,
Running!
To my first love!

I repent for where I went astray,
Where my ears were covered
And my eyes were blind -
I lay my pride down at the altar.

I declare God is my salvation!
I will trust.
I will not be afraid.
I declare He is my strength and my song.

My lamp stand will not be removed
As I come before You - humble, repentant,
And wholeheartedly declare:

I will not leave, forsake, or abandon You

My Lord,
My Savior,
My God,
Yahweh,
My first love.

*PSALM 73:25, JOHN 15:13, PSALM 16:2, REVELATION 2:4, 1 JOHN
4:19, PSALM 91:2, ISAIAH 12:2, 1 JOHN 4:10, REVELATION 2:5,
JEREMIAH 1:5, PSALM 139:6*

DECLARATION OF SALT

I declare that the words that leave my lips
Will be full of compassion,
Preserving the holiness of His Word,
And seasoning the Earth with the salt
Of the uncompromised Truths
Of His Kingdom.

COLOSSIANS 4:6

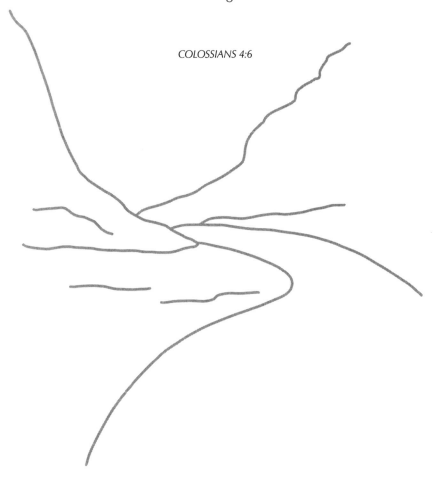

DECLARATION OF HUMILITY

I lay down my pride at His altar,
letting the flames of His humble glory
consume all pride within me.

I declare that rest for my soul resides in
placing His yoke up my shoulders,
it is light, it is easy, it is guiding my feet in humility.

I declare the whispers of serenity and gentleness of my Savior
speak louder than
any shouts of earthly glory and power by the Enemy.

I declare I am a child of meekness,
choosing to go lower still,
joyfully living in this upside down kingdom
where the last shall be first, and the first shall be last.

I declare humility wells up in my spirit
and I live to faithfully follow in the steps
of my humble King, Yeshua.

MATTHEW 11:29, MATTHEW 5:5, PSALM 37:11, 2 CORINTHIANS 10:1

DECREE OF THE PIONEER SPIRIT

I declare I am
A Pioneer,
A Trailblazer,
A Forerunner
Called, equipped, and sent forth by the Spirit of the living God
To recognize the new things,
To blaze the road in the wilderness,
To call forth the streams in the wasteland .

My destiny scroll is marked with the
Stamp of forerunner,
Trusted pioneer for Yahweh!

I declare no howling in the wilderness will stop me,
For the lamp of His Word will light my path,
The cloud of His presence in the day
And the pillar of His fire by night.

I declare my gaze is fixed on Yeshua,
Who is the Author and the Perfecter of my faith
The ultimate Pioneer -
I declare my feet will not slip - no matter the terrain.
I declare my mind will not wander - no matter the onslaught.

I declare the banner of breakthrough fervently waves over my life,
Dipped in the blood of the Lamb,
Victory is in Yeshua!

I declare I pioneer into the unknown for Him!

Breath to dry bones
Living waters to barren deserts
Peace into cracks of chaos
Direction into the lost
Ways where there are no ways!

I declare I will finish the race
No matter the canyon, the valley or the mountaintop.
I will run with Truth at my right
And Spirit at my left.

For the Word of God is my sword,
For the Peace of God is my compass,
For the Love of God is my shield,
For the Holiness of God is a cloak over me.

I declare I am a PIONEER for Yahweh,
My reward cannot be given by this world!

Just as the angels cry out
Holy, Holy, Holy
My soul cries
Holy, Holy, Holy!
And the great cloud of witnesses embrace me,
Echoing the destiny set forth before me:

Pioneer, trailblazer, forerunner.

I declare I will pioneer,
I will forerun,
I will trailblaze
This great race set before me.

ISAIAH 43;19, JOSHUA 3:4-5

DECREE OF RIGHTEOUSNESS AND JUSTICE

I declare a reawakening of the
Justice of Heaven
And the Righteousness of Yahweh
Within my soul
Within my family
Within the highest courts of law in my nation!

I declare I will stand when others bow
To rise when others fall away
And to declare life when the world is speaking death.

I break every lying spirit that has tried to
Distract, discourage, and discredit
The spirit of justice and righteousness
That is my birthright as a son or daughter of the Most High.

I declare
Righteousness and justice are the foundation of Your throne;
Love and faithfulness go before You
And surround me, my family, and my blood line.

I declare my family will
Never be stricken with panic.
My feet are planted upon the tested Stone
The sure foundation
The precious cornerstone.

I declare I am a sower of light.
Irrepressible joy swells with me
Because of who and whose I am.

My life is marked by
His favor and His protection

I declare the mighty Justice and
The unwavering Righteousness
Of the One who is and is to come

I declare you
Are LORD,
Yahweh,
That is your name!
All glory and splendor are yours!

I declare the mighty rains of justice,
The roaring thunders of righteousness,
And the majestic flashes of Your glory
Come down upon
The evil schemes,
The unjust statutes,
Oppressive decrees,
And the graven images that
Have stolen Your glory and praise!

By Your strong right hand
I declare the destruction of demonic strongholds,
And a tsunami of the uncompromisingly righteous
To sweep across the nations!

I declare He is faithful to all generations.
His faithfulness flows from the Justice and Righteousness His throne sits upon.

I declare Our Father, Our King, the God of Angel Armies
Is a lover of Justice
He is right,
Just
And fair in all His ways.

PSALM 89:14, ISAIAH 42:8, PSALM 97:2, PSALM 97:6,
PSALM 89:9, ISAIAH 10:1-2

DECLARATION OF
THE SECRET PLACE

I declare I live to pray the prayers of the secret place,
Prostrate before you,
Hidden in your Shadow,
Abiding in the rooms of your Kingdom,
My prayers and thanksgivings lifted before you as a living sacrifice.

I declare my joy is to rest in the quiet rooms of Your heart,
The door closed, the outpourings of my spirit entering
Into the realm of the unseen where my Heavenly Father resides.

I decree the prayers I pray in the secret place
Will flood the public streets of my life with the fruit of Heaven.

I declare my Father sees me,
Listening,
Watching,
And the prayers of the secret place delight the heart of my Father.

MATTHEW 6:5-6, JAMES 1:21

DECLARATION OF
HIS GLORY

I declare I have seen His glory
Full of Grace and Truth,
The glory of the one and the only Son,
Who came from the Father.
I declare His glory across humanity,
Sweeping through the darkness with marvelous light;
To my God and Father be the glory forever and ever.
I declare I will arise,
I declare I will shine,
With the marvelous glory of the Lord
for my Light has come,
And the glory of the King rises upon me!

PHILIPPIANS 4:20, PSALM 57:5, LUKE 2:14,
ISAIAH 60:1, 2 CORINTHIANS 3:18

DECLARATION OF THE KEYS OF THE KINGDOM

I declare I have been given indisputable authority,
the very keys of the Kingdom of Heaven!

Whatever I bind on earth will be bound in heaven,
and whatever I loose on earth will be loosed in heaven!

I declare the key is in my hand
and as I step into this Glory set before me,
I declare in the name of Jesus that every open demonic door in my life:
be closed now!!

I bind the strong man and plunder his house
and his goods by the blood of Jesus!

Satan, I bind you from this region,
I bind you from my life - my family - and my physical body!
I break every agreement in my generational line!
I renounce every sacrifice and false covenant offered by me or my ancestors!

I declare the strong man is bound and his house is plundered, destroyed, and
never to be built again, in Jesus name!

I bind the Leviathan spirit,
I declare a hook in Leviathan's jaw by the Spirit of God - and all prideful, blocking, haughty spirits of intimidation and fear removed from my life!
I declare my God has crushed the heads of Leviathan
and given him as food to the creatures of the wilderness!

I bind all curses and spirits of sickness, disease, infirmity, and death that have
been released against my body in the name of Jesus!
Every spirit of darkness assigned to my will and emotions,
be bound now and never return!
I declare the blood of Jesus from the top of my head to the soles of my feet and
an infilling of the Holy Spirit in every vacant part of my being.

Again I take up the key, and I decree the opening of the doors over my life
to the blessings of the Kingdom of God: be open now!!

I loose the joy of the Lord,
I declare a double portion of joy!
a double portion of grace!

I declare a release of the fruits of the spirit:
love, joy, peace, patience, kindness, generosity, faithfulness, gentleness, and
self-control!

I loose the love of God over myself
and my entire family line!
I declare I receive it, Lord!

I receive the key to the house of David and declare what the Lord opens
no one can shut, and what He shuts, no one can open.

I receive my destiny scroll with boldness, courage, and strength!

I declare the words of John

"When I saw Him, I fell at His feet like a dead man.
But he placed His right hand on me and said 'Do not be afraid.
I am the first and the Last, The Living One, I was dead and behold,
Now I am alive forever and ever.
And I hold the keys of Death and Hades!'"

I declare He is alive - for evermore!

MATTHEW 16:19, PSALM 74:13,
REVELATION 1:18-19,
MATTHEW 18:18, PSALM 94

DECLARATION OF LIGHT

I declare I am a child of the Kingdom of Light,
The Lord is my light and my salvation.

I declare darkness has no place in my destiny,
For I am a child of light,
Called forth by the very Light of life, Jesus.

I declare I am the light of the world,
A city set upon a hill,
And I will shine in the depths of darkness,
His word a lamp unto my feet and a
Light unto my path.

I declare God is light and in
Him there is no darkness at all.

Hallelujah!

JOHN 8:12, 1 JOHN 1:5,
JOHN 1:5, 1 PETER 2:9,
MATTHEW 5:14 4:6

DECLARATION OF SONSHIP

I declare the Spirit of my Father gives witness to my spirit:
I am His child, beloved and treasured.
I declare my identity rests in His Kingdom.
I am His child, unique and powerful.

I declare peace abounds within me,
for there is no striving and no performance
within the family of God.

I declare I live to know Him
and He created me to know me.

I declare the mindset of sonship over my thought process,
with ears to hear the testimony of the Spirit of Lord:
the Spirit of knowledge, wisdom and understanding,
the Spirit of counsel, power and fear of the Lord.

I declare the Spirit of adoption rises up within me,
defeating any and all orphan spirits twisting the destiny call of my life.

I declare I am no longer a slave!

I declare all counterfeit voices to be silenced,
and a release of my spiritual destiny as a child of the Most High!

I declare I am known by my Father,
His Spirit gives witness to my Spirit,
I am His,
chosen to live,
to breathe,
and to walk the Earth for such a time as this.

EPHESIANS 1:5, ROMANS 8:15, ROMANS 8:16, GALATIANS 4:6

69

MOUNTAINS
OF LIFE

The ascent up the rugged, unpredictable mountains of life - some steeper and some harsher than others. Chaos. Despair. Hopelessness. Loneliness. The terrain can be unforgiving, testing every part of your willpower and shaking the very foundations of your faith. One foot in front of the other, you climb - in the wind, in the rain, in the sun, in the snow. The enemy will lie, whispering the unattainability of the promise, but you keep going just as David did, leaning into the name of Yahweh.

The mountains can be steep, but don't let the ascent intimidate you. He has deposited within you the authority and power to speak to the mountain - and it will move. The decrees leave your mouth, as arrows of light consuming the darkness pressing around you and releasing the glorious radiance of His promised rescue and peace.

He has never left you, He will never leave you. He is with you to the end of the ages. These mountains will be stones in your sling. His banner waves over you.

He is Jehovah Nissi.

DECLARATION TO TRAMPLE HELL

I declare I have been given the freedom and authority,
To trample and tread on snakes, scorpions, and Satan himself!

I call my spirit to attention and
Step into the delegated authority and influence
Offered to me by Jesus Christ!

I declare I will overcome
All the power,
All the influence,
And all the forces of the Devil.

And I declare
Nothing - will harm me!
Nothing - will injure me!
Nothing - will act unjustly towards me!

I possess the Authority given to me
By the Word who is Yeshua,
My wondrous King Jesus,
Who is the Lion and the Lamb!

I declare over my life and the generations to come -
Crush Hell!
Overcome darkness!
And walk in the
Freedom, power, and authority of Christ Jesus!

LUKE 10:19

DECLARATION OF VICTORY

I declare He is the Lord my God
And He goes with me,
In every battle and every war,
Fighting against every demonic spirit sent against me!

I declare He gives me victory over every spirit of darkness.

PSALM 34:17, ISAIAH 41:11

DECREE TO BREAK DELAYS

I declare there is a divinely appointed time for the plans of my life,
I am patient and trusting, even in the lingering!
I am humble in heart, posturing myself in faith before you -
Almighty Father, You reign supreme!

I declare with unwavering confidence to every deceiving and lying spirit
sent to distract me from my destiny,
My God has heard my prayers and
He is actively working on my behalf!

I speak to every unjust spirit of delay attached to my life - I declare be
broken now by the Spirit of God!
I declare the fiery justice of Yahweh upon any demonic adversaries that
have been sent to delay, stall, and frustrate
the plans of God for my life.

I declare my trust, my hope and my strength is in the Lord who will
promptly carry out justice on my behalf!
I declare I am the head - and not the tail - and every delaying spirit sent to
postpone my future, I rebuke you by the blood of Jesus!

I declare supernatural strength over myself to stand,
just as Daniel stood - every opposing spirit be shattered!
for my God, the Great I Am, always answers!

LUKE 18:1, HABAKKUK 2:3, DANIEL 10:12-13

DECREE OF NEW WINE

I declare a new wine!
I refuse to carry the old wineskin,
Full of spirits of religion, legalism, and control.
Be bound in the name of Jesus -
I declare you cannot live in this new wine!

I declare a new wine and a new wineskin is my hands!
Ripe with revival,
With healing,
With spiritual freedom,
With child-like faith,
And with Holy Spirit breathed power and authority!

I declare my feet are stepping into the new vineyard,
And I trust the Chief Vinedresser
The keeper of the vineyard,
For his hands are gentle,
And His pruning sheers alive with the
Living, breathing words of Jesus,
Yes, Jesus!

He is the Lord my God
Who brings me into a promised land,
Gifting me cities I did not build,
Houses full of blessings I did not earn,
Wells I did not dig,
Vineyards I did not tend,
Olive trees I did not plant!

I decree Faith to remain in the field,
Courage to put my hands to work,
And Spiritual maturity to see the Harvest.

I declare I am a joy-filled worker of the vineyard:
Even in the pressing,
I am not crushed.
Even when there looks to be no way out,
I am not in despair.
Even in the persecution,
I am not forsaken.
Even when I am struck down,
I am not destroyed.

I declare an outpouring of the new wine across humanity,
And for the seeds of the Gospel to be brought to an accelerated maturation!

I call in the harvest of souls,
I call in the new wine!

I'm a worker in the field,
And I carry in my own body the death of Jesus
So that the life of Jesus may be also revealed!

I declare break out the oil,
Ready the new wine,
Set the table,
It is harvest time!

*JOHN 18:1-2, MARK 14:34, 2 CORINTHIANS 4:8-9,
MARK 2:22, LUKE 5:37, DEUTERONOMY 6:11-13*

DECREE OVER CULTURE

I declare a kingdom shift in culture:
A renewal of minds,
A removal of demonic strongholds over eyes and ears,
And a righteous refusal of hearts to be conformed to the ways of this world.

I decree the devil no longer has control of the highest places,
I declare the zeal of God's people to go forth,
Tearing down, in the spirit and the natural, every false altar built upon a mountain of culture.

I declare His Name above all names, and opening of the hearts of humanity:

"For God so loved the world, that He gave His only Son, that anyone who believes in Him should not die but have eternal life."

I declare the Spirit of the throne of God:
Righteousness and Justice to invade the spirits of all who sit upon these influential mountaintops.

I declare clean hearts, renewed spirits.

Jesus reigns.

ROMANS 12:2, PSALM 51:10

DECLARATION OF WAITING ON THE LORD

I declare I wait for the Lord,
I am not moved by the shifting
pressures of culture,
I trust His timing, His movements.

For my hope lives and finds life in His Word!
I deeply desire the weightiness of His presence,
More than a watchman waiting for morning,
I declare I wait, I long,
And I hope in the Lord -
Even more than a watchman
waiting for morning!

I declare I am secure in His promise -
waiting for my King.

PSALM 130:6

DECREE OVER RELIGION

I declare I was not created to live within the chains of religion!

I declare the dethroning of the spirit of religion in my life;
Where the spirit of the Lord is there is freedom!

I declare I was born to be in relationship with Him,
His love for me is not dictated by the striving of my hands.
Where legalistic lies have created a hardness in my heart,
I declare a softening by the agape love of Abba Father.

I declare the spirit of performance no longer has
A voice in my relationship with Jesus,
I release myself from the lies of formula and works,
And I throw off the suffocating blanket of religion
Void of love, joy, and relationship.

I declare the Lord calls me His Beloved,
Not because of my gifting and talents,
But because of who He created me to be!

I declare all cynicism and hypercritical spirits that have paraded
around as Discernment be broken off my destiny and
For a flood of holy, divine revelation
From the Heart of the Father to come over my life.

I declare a release of the healing joy of Heaven over every
Wounding and hurt caused by religious leaders, and I declare the
spirit of obligation has no voice in my relationship
with the King.

Every dam built by the religious spirit, break now!
I declare a flooding of my spirit with the Living Waters of Jesus,
Washing away any and all pain and deception and releasing my
destiny as a child of the King.

I declare I will no longer live a life controlled
By the spirit of religion,
The Holy Spirit knows me,
Jesus loves me,
The Father delights over me.

I declare relationship over religion!

ROMANS 8:9, JOHN 14:26, ROMANS 8:14, ROMANS 8:16

DECREE TO RUN

I decree a divine removal of every demonic arrow of
Betrayal, unforgiveness, shame, and pain.
I declare I will run my race without a limp,
I let go of the wounding and receive the healing balm of Heaven.

HEBREWS 12:1

DECREE TO PERSIST AND FINSH

I declare a fresh breath of holy endurance fills my lungs,
a desire to persist in cheerful steadfastness,
no matter the course, no matter the road, no matter the obstacles!

I declare the Lord of Heaven's Armies speaks
a word of encouragement over my life:
"Be Strong and finish the task!"

I decree "Yes!" unto the One who sits in the Heavens.

A tenacity of spirit lives within me because of Him,
inspiring me to run, to persist, and to finish the race set before me!

I declare I will persist,
with footsteps
devoted to prayer,
with a heart rejoicing in hope,
and with a spirit
persevering in tribulation.

I declare I am not alone,
for He has given me the Holy Spirit,
and He runs beside me!

JAMES 1:4, ROMANS 12:12, ZECHARIAH 8:9

DECLARATION OF LIBERTY

I declare I am free;
the body and blood of Jesus paid for
everything that the law could not.

ACTS 13:39

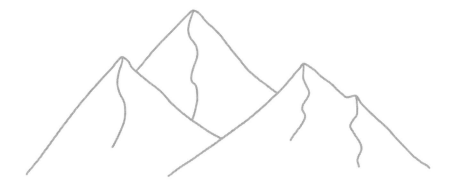

DECLARATION
OF REBUILDING

I declare the day of rebuilding will come,
A strengthening of my walls,
An extension of my boundaries.

What the enemy tore down will be rebuilt.

I declare the day of rebuilding is coming.

MICAH 7:11

DECREE OF A PROMISE

I declare He is Faithful,
faithful to fulfill the promise!

I declare to the lies wrapped in the whisperings of
the minutes, the days, and the years:

He who promised is faithful.
He who promised is faithful.

I declare my spirit holds tightly to the One who knit me in my mother's womb.
I heard his voice as he called to me, imparting to my spirit plans of
prosperity, hope, and a future. I declare He is faithful to fulfill the promise!

I declare my promise is wrapped in unwavering hope in the Lord,
renewing my strength and lifting me to soar on wings like eagles.

I declare I will continue to walk in the peace of the promise,
weariness will not control me.

I decree faithful is the voice of Yahweh who calls to me.
I declare He will do it, fulfilling His call in my life,
marking me with holiness, protecting me with righteousness,
watching over me, for I am His own.

I declare my hope lives in the testimonies of His promises,
and I am not swayed by the reality that surrounds me.

I declare His name reigns,
above my promise,
above my desires,
and I live to glorify Him in the pursuit of the promise.

My promise is guarded by Yahweh.

He who promised is faithful.

MATTHEW 28:20,
ISAIAH 40:31,
JEREMIAH 29:11,
1 THESSALONIANS 5:24,
HEBREWS 10:23

DECLARATION
OF FORGIVENESS

I declare I will forgive, just as the Lord forgave me.
I am a child of grace, not a child of a grudge.
I declare the sting of betrayal and hurt will no longer speak
louder than the words of Jesus:

"Forgive us of our sins, as we forgive those
who have sinned against us."

I declare my battle is not with flesh and blood,
and I lay all hurt, offense, and anger down
at the feet of Jesus.

I release myself from carrying the burden of unforgiveness, not
excusing what was done, but choosing to let
the Lord carry it for me.

I declare my life is not defined by offense,
but rather by His spirit of forgiveness and love.

I declare I am tenderhearted, abounding in forgiveness,
and I choose to live in the freedom of the riches of His Grace.

EPHESIANS 4:32, MARK 11:25, EPHESIANS 1:7

DECLARATION
OF OVERCOMING

I declare I am an overcomer.
Victory lives within me
Because of who created me.
I am born of God
Crafted by God
And created by God.

I declare I will not be overcome by evil,
But I will overcome evil with good.

I declare He is the overcomer of the world.
And I receive the victory He authored
Through His son.
Greater is He in me
than he that is in this world.

*ROMANS 12:21, 1 JOHN
5:4, REVELATION 3:21,
1 JOHN 5:5, REVELATION
3:5, REVELATION 2:7*

DECREE OF
IDENTITY

I declare I was purposely created,
Knitted together,
Formed in my mother's womb,
And set apart

I declare I am clothed in the robes of
Compassion,
Kindness,
Humility,
Meekness,
And patience.

My heart beats to the rhythm of the Kingdom,
And I declare the plans God has breathed out over my life
Are good, wrapped in delight,
With a destiny saturated in radical hope and unfettered joy.

I declare the carnal life I was born into is dead
And my new life is hidden in Christ Jesus,
Marked by the blood and body of the One who
Suffered, died and rose again to forever graft
Me as a citizen of Heaven,
And sealed with the promised Holy Spirit.

I am a new creation in Him - and I declare the new has come!

I decree the demonic forces of Hell have no legal right to
My identity
My mind
My emotions
My family
My future
My health
Or my dreams.
I am a blood-bought child, and the Kingdom of Heaven
Shouts holy and beloved over the breaths of life in my lungs.

Declarations of light and life rise up within me
Because before I was even formed in the womb
I was appointed - a royal priesthood, a holy nation chosen by Yahweh himself.

I speak to my spirit and say:

Prophesy Truth,
Preach the Good News,
Heal the sick,
Trample on Hell,
Call the prodigals home,
Pick up your torch and carry it with the authority given to you
By the one who saw Satan fall like lightning from Heaven!

From the North, the South, the West, and the East
I decree dry bones to life!

I declare no darkness shall never dim the marvelous light which burns
morning, noon, and night within me.

I declare I am His.
Forever.
And no scheme, no plot, no cultural lie of the enemy,
will ever snatch me from His strong right hand.

I declare the fingerprint of the Almighty,
the Father of Lights,
protects me and delights over my life.

*EPHESIANS 1:13, 2 CORINTHIANS 5:17, JEREMIAH
1:5, 1 PETER 2:9, JEREMIAH 29:11, COLOSSIANS 3:12,
COLOSSIANS 3:3*

DECREE OF HOLINESS

I declare I have been called,
summoned unto the servanthood of the Most High,
to step into the Garden of Faith,
arming myself with prayer - night and day:
overcoming every form of evil as a victorious soldier
of Jesus, the Anointed one!

I decree a greater release of God's grace, His love,
His total well-being to flow into my life from my Father,
and from my Lord, Jesus Christ!

I declare strong, firm faith,
to be passed down through my family line -
faith that requires the leaning of my entire personality on God in Christ:
in absolute trust,
in steadfast confidence,
in His power,
in His wisdom,
and in His goodness.

I declare He is my life-giver,
calling,
confirming,
drawing me in,
and delighting in me before time even began!

I declare I have been given the gift of resurrection life,
by the one who annulled death,
who dismantled death - Yes, Jesus!
I declare He has obliterated all effects of death in my life,
and His immortal life lives within me through the Gospel!

I declare I have been called into holiness,
a life of consecration to further the Gospel,
and He has anointed me as His preacher,
as His apostle,
and His teacher of Truth
to the nations.

I declare faith,
I declare confidence,
I declare an unwavering flame of belief burns inside of me
Setting ablaze all shame, all unworthiness, all lies of the Evil one.
For I am convinced, that all I've placed in His hands is
safe and secure until His return.

I decree:
Awaken the flames, Lord,
fan the fire of the Spirit of God,
stir up the gift of God within me,
rekindle the embers - excite the fire,
the sacred fire of the precious Holy Spirit!

I declare a wildfire of faith burns with me -
and the waters of this world cannot
and will not quench it.

2 TIMOTHY 1:11, 1 PETER 3:4, 2 CORINTHIANS 4:16, PROVERBS 10:6

DECLARATION OF THE
ESSENCE OF THE KINGDOM

I declare a mighty torrent
Of the wind of your spirit,
The breath of your kingdom,
And the peace of your throne
To fall upon on me.

PSALM 4:8

DECREE OF STRENGTH

I declare I will not live in the stronghold of fear and anxiety.

Spirit of fear, I break your hold on my life,
I declare I will not be dismayed!
Spirit of anxiety, I bind you from my life,
I declare I am delivered and set free!

I declare my God is mighty,
He strengthens me, He helps me, He upholds me,
There is no worldly power that can prevail
Against the strength of His powerful righteous hand.

I declare my confidence is founded in the
Unmovable, unchangeable, all-powerful Rock of the Ages.
He lifts me high above the snares of the enemy.

I declare Hell has no legal hold on me,
I break every attack sent against me and my family
By the body and blood of the Savior of the world
Yeshua the Messiah.

I bind to my mind the words of Jesus:
"Take heart; it is I, have no fear."

I declare I will walk through the
valley of the shadow of death!
I will not sit down or succumb to the depths of the valley!

I declare I will move forward confidently following His rod and His staff.

Evil will not touch me,
For Adonai is with me.

ISAIAH 41:10, 1 PETER 5:7,
JOHN 14:27, PHILIPPIANS
4:6-7, PSALM 34;4, PSALM
23:4, MATTHEW 14:27

DECLARATION OF FAITH

I declare faith!
Belief in Him
The Great I am, who was, who is, and is to come!

I speak to every ounce of disbelief in my
Heart, mind, and body and I declare
Be consumed with
Faith,
Belief,
Trust,
Confidence,
Fidelity,
Faithfulness.

I declare to the mountain before me
Move -
I declare to the diagnosis before me
Move -
I declare to the sickness before me -
Move -
I declare to the doubt before me -
Move -

I declare nothing will be impossible with my God,
For I have chosen Him
And He has always chosen me.

Torrents of living water flow from me!
And as I walk,
I walk in faith,
Triumphantly walking down
The path of The Way.

I declare faith in this place!
And decree to every dead and despairing spirit
Awake!
Let there be water in the wilderness
And streams in the desert!

I call my Spirit to attention
And my ears to listen to the voice of victory of my King Jesus who says,

"Don't be afraid - Just believe!"

I declare my Faith does not rest in the wisdom of men
but in the power of God!

I declare a deposit of faith to fall,
I ask just as the apostles did "Increase our faith!"

I declare I have chosen the way of Faithfulness -
I am on guard. Firm in faith. Courageous. Strong.

I declare that I will fear not,
For He is with me.
I stand in faith, leaning on His strength
And upheld by His righteous right hand.

I declare that surely
I have a future
And my hope
Will not
Be cut off.

ISAIAH 35:6 JOHN 7:38, MARK 5:36, ROMANS 10:17, 2
CORINTHIANS 5:7, GALATIANS 2:16,
MARK 11:22-24, LUKE 1:37, 1 CORINTHIANS 2:5,
1 CORINTHIANS 16:13, PSALM 119:30, ROMANS 1:17,
LUKE 17:5, PROVERBS 23:18, ISAIAH 41:10

DECREE OF GOD WARRING

I declare I serve a mighty, Holy, and righteous King.
He is the Deliverer - and He fights for me!

When the enemy comes in like a flood,
The Spirit of the Lord Jehovah rises up and crushes him!

The Lord Yahweh is His name!
He is glorious in power!
He is like a mighty warrior!
His zeal is like a man of war!

I declare He guards my feet as I stand firmly
On foundations of righteousness and justice.
I do not waiver at the onslaughts of the enemy because He surrounds me -
I declare He will contend with all who contend with me,
For the Lord Yahweh is His name!

I declare He will fight for me - and I will hold my peace!
I am strong, courageous;
No fear or dismay is within me because
My Lord, My God, goes before me as a consuming fire,
And also behind me - protecting me with His strong right arm.
His thunderings from the Heavens breaks my adversaries into pieces!

I declare His favor upon my life,
The favor of the Almighty Warrior King -
Who exalts the horn of His anointed
And makes the crooked paths straight!

I declare I am anointed for such a time as this!
I will rise - in courage!
I will stand - in victory!
I will pray - in power and authority!
I will decree - and it shall be established!

And when the enemy strikes, he will be defeated!
Not by my own sword, but by God's right hand
And the very light of His countenance!

I declare the cries of the Righteous are heard!
Every prayer and petition does not fall on deaf ears,
For the Lord who is strong in battle
Listens,
Responds,
And delivers.

I declare He is Mighty - and He is with me.

*ISAIAH 59:19, PSALM 34:17, ISAIAH 41:11, 1 SAMUEL 2:9-10, ISAIAH 42:13, ISAIAH 45:2,
ISAIAH 52:12, DEUTERONOMY 9:3, EXODUS 14:14, ISAIAH 49:25, JEREMIAH 1:8*

DECLARATION OF A NEW YEAR

I declare my family and I will
Serve the Lord.

The Lord will heal my household:
Minds, Bodies, Relationships, and Brokenness.

I declare my family will
Run, dance, and rejoice
In the land of the living -

Death and sickness have no right,
Over my family or generational line.

My health was paid for by the stripes of my Savior,
I declare His Body and His Blood speak a better word!

I declare rest and peace will surround my house.

JOSHUA 24:15

DECREE OF THE FRIENDSHIP OF GOD

I declare I was created to be in friendship with Him,
The Almighty yet Loving Father.
His Lamp shines above my head,
The Light of Yahweh,
Guiding me as I walk,
Through dark paths,
Through dim valleys,
Gently leading me to a meadow of safety,
Where the friendship of God rests upon my tent.

JOB 29:3-4

DECREE OF THE CHAMPION

I declare the spirit of the champion lives with me,
His banner of victory wraps around me.
My victory lives in the drops of blood poured out for me.
I declare He is the champion living within me.

ROMANS 8:37, 1 CORINTHIANS 15:57

DECLARATION OF BOLDNESS LIKE A LION

I declare I am created and destined to live in boldness,
to thrive in a lifestyle of assurance in Jesus!

I declare this gift of boldness does not come from this world -
it is born from on high and answers to no man or law,
it is a divine gift imparted to my spirit from the Realm of Yahweh!

I decree this boldness from above
straightens my spine,
crushes my fears,
opens my mouth,
moves my feet
and transforms
my family,
my city,
my nation,
and the world!

I declare I was created
to proclaim and teach the Kingdom of God
with all boldness
with all certainty
and without hindrance!

I decree I am bold,
I decree I am courageous,
no fear of conflict, no fear of man,
no spirit of intimidation will stop me
from boldly declaring the Good News,
from boldly standing for Righteousness!

ACTS 28:31, 1 THESSALONIANS 2:2,
HEBREWS 10:19, 2 CORINTHIANS 3:12, ACTS 4:31, 2 CORINTHIANS 7:4,
2 TIMOTHY 1:6, PROVERBS 28:1

For Yeshua, Jesus,
the Lion of Judah,
roars with me, overwhelming me with boldness
and acts of wickedness, evil, and unrighteousness
do not happen without my righteous pursuit!

I declare my prayers are powerful
and I pray with a bold tongue - with 100% assurance in Divine Truth.

I declare I am not drowning in the waves of religious law!
I am free, joyfully swimming in an ocean of boldness -
not by my power or might but because of the blood of Yeshua!

Just as the Holy Spirit shook the walls of the Upper Room,
I declare He shakes within me, the Chieftain of Boldness,
the mighty Holy Spirit, filling, empowering, and allowing me
to speak the word of God with boldness everywhere I go!

I declare my spirit is bold, filled with faith and confidence
to see the sick healed,
to see the lost found,
to see the prodigals return,
to see Truth triumph,
to see all nations
hear, receive, and be transformed by the living,
breathing power of the only name, Jesus!

I declare I have hope that flows from on high,
and because of that hope, I have boldness from on high
that cannot ever be taken from me!

I declare a bold shout of the name of Jesus
into my family and my generational line,
and a fanning into flame the gift of God that is in me!

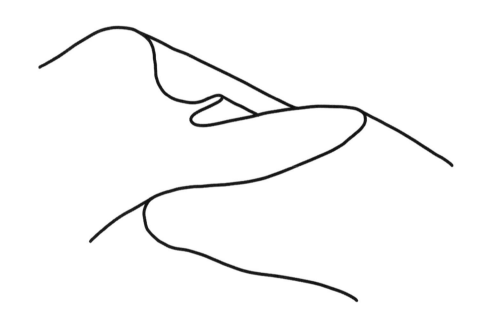

MANNA
IN THE WILD

It's the moment of deep pressing: mind, body, soul. You've walked as far as you can - striving, believing, pushing beyond what you thought you could. The brutality of the wild desert season has exhausted all familiar and worldly options for rescue and renewal. Deliverance no longer rests in the solutions of the past, a return to Egypt is no longer the answer.

Your only hope lives in Him.
Fire by night,
Cloud by day,
Bread from heaven,
Water from a rock.
Let the manna cover the desert.

It is time to decree, to release a word wrapped in the Holy Scriptures, that goes before you riding on the wings of faith, partnering with the promises of His ever faithful, ever present, ever powerful name.

He is Lord Yahweh.

DECLARATION TO YESHUA

I declare I belong to Yeshua,
Mind, body, and soul,
A heart that receives You,
Ears that hear You,
Eyes that see You,
Feet that walk with You,
Lips that praise You,
Imagination that adores You,
Hands that hold You,
Arms that embrace You,
Lungs that breathe You,
A smile that reflects You,
A generational line that follows You.
I declare I belong to Yeshua.

JOHN 3:16

DECREE OF THE BODY AND BLOOD OF JESUS

I declare a Holy Moment,
Remembering Jesus
As He sat in the Upper Room with His twelve and said:

"Do this in remembrance of me"

I am here now,
Making a decree of the Victory of Your Body, of Your Blood,
Remembering what You did for me!

I declare there is nothing more powerful,
Than the body and blood of my Savior,
I declare Jesus,
My King,
Personally and willingly
Took my sins and carried
Them on His body
To the cross.

Every curse, every sickness, every tormenting spirit,
Even death itself was defeated upon the cross!

I declare I am cleansed and covered
By the Blood of Jesus, and the destroyer Satan cannot touch me!

I declare I am immune to the penalty and the power of sin
Because of His Body broken,
His blood poured out,
His offering of Himself as an altar of sacrifice
- For me and all of humanity!

I declare I believe:

By Your stripes,
I am healed.

By Your bread,
I will live forever.

By Your blood,
I am washed clean, walking in freedom.

By Your punishment,
I live in peace.

By Your death and resurrection,
I spend Eternity with You.

By the precious blood of the sinless, spotless Lamb,
I am redeemed, living for righteousness.

I declare I live in the new covenant,
Paid for with the body and blood of Jesus!

I declare
Life-saving,
Life-changing,
Destiny-transforming
Power
In the Blood and the Body of Jesus!

HEBREW 11:28,
REVELATION 12:11,
1 PETER 18-19,
1 CORINTHIANS 11:23-26,
1 PETER 2:24,
HEBREWS 9:22,
1 PETER 2:22

DECLARATION OF FIRE AND WATER

I declare I will not be overcome
by fear,
by rising waters,
by fiery flames,
for He is with me.

I declare He knows me,
calling me by name,
and decreeing a shield of protection over me.

I declare I will pass through the waters,
I will not drown.
I declare I will go through the rivers,
I will not be swept away.
I declare I will walk through the fires,
I will not be scorched.

I declare the perils of this world are no match for My Father,
for He is with me and has redeemed me.

ISAIAH 43:1-2

DECREE OF MY HIDING PLACE

I declare you are my hiding place,
I rest in your covering,
I thrive under your protection.

I declare I am surrounded with a ringing cry from the Heavenlies,
Releasing melodious songs of deliverance:
Alive with righteousness and salvation
PSALM 32:7
That surround me,
Cover me,
And protect me from trouble.

I declare I am hidden in Him.

Selah.

DECREE OF MY RESTING PLACE

I declare He is my shelter,
His safe arms around me,
protecting me from those who are against me
with His faithful shield of majesty and glory.

PSALM 91:4

DECLARATION OF MY FRIEND HOLY SPIRIT

I declare I have a good Father who gives good gifts -
And He has given me an eternal friend,
Power from above
The promised Holy Spirit:

My Comforter,
Near to me in grief and suffering.

My Counselor,
Teaching and leading me in all things.

My Helper,
Forever by my side in the mountains and the valleys.

My Intercessor,
Lifting the groans of my human frailty to the ears of the Father.

My Advocate,
Warring and strengthening me as we stand, together,
against the lies of the Destroyer.

I declare I am never alone
- even in moments of despair and weariness -
He is there.

I declare I have the power
To pull down strongholds,
To bind and restrict the enemy,
Because of the fire of the Holy Spirit
That burns within me
And the blood of Jesus that covers me!

Flames of fire dance upon me
As I worship God in Spirit and Truth
Triumphantly walking beside by the Spirit of God because I am a child of God!

I declare the success of my life is not
Measured by the shifting sands of this world!

I declare my body is the very sanctuary of the Holy Spirit,
A treasured gift from God, bursting with the fruit of the Spirit:

Love, joy, peace, patience, kindness, goodness,
faithfulness, gentleness and self control!

I declare I overflow with hope,
And my very breath changes atmospheres.

I declare I walk in boldness
where many have cowered and bowed their knee;
I rise up and walk as the Holy Spirit backs me in confidence and power.

He is my intimate friend,
Filling my mouth with purposed kingdom declarations of truth and freedom.
I declare the Holy Spirit
Loves to be in friendship with me.

He is the Spirit-Wind,
Falling upon all of humanity
The spirit of Holiness,
Breaking the twisted lies of the world.

I declare the Holy Spirit
is my covenant promise from Lord Yahweh!
Resting on me in fire and glory.

*ISAIAH 59:21, JOHN 14:26,
1 CORINTHIANS 6:19-20,
ROMANS 8:14,
ROMANS 15:13, LUKE 11:13*

DECREE OF JOY

I declare my path of life is paved with
the gleaming joy of Your presence, the shining glory of Your face!

The mutterings of the happiness of the flesh are fleeting -
I declare my joy, is solid, unwavering, fixed upon the Rock
that is higher than I.
I declare I am infused with joy.
My spirit receives the words of my Savior who spoke,

"If you keep my commands,
You will remain in my love,
Just as I have kept my Father's commands
And remain in His love.
I have told you this so that my joy may be in you
and your joy may be complete."

I declare the joy of the very Savior of Humanity
Yeshua
is flowing within me!

The one who
suffered for me,
was ridiculed for me,
died for me,
and rose again for me -
I declare His joy,
the joy paid for with body and blood,
is flourishing
and overflowing within me.

I decree streams of
calm delight
course through me,
washing over every cell of my body
and overflowing into every conversation, situation,
and journey set before me.

I declare my mouth is a mouth of Jubilee,
singing forth shouts of joy,
wrapped in peace, and dripping with hope by the power of the Holy Spirit!
Rejoice! He is alive!

I declare as I go out in joy and am led forth in peace,
the mountains and hills will burst into song before me
and all the trees of the field will clap their hands!

I declare an eviction of this tenant known as weeping.
Your evening stay is over - leave!
For the joy of the morning is here!
Just as the sun burst forth at the dawn of Easter - I decree a shout of joy,
for the King arrayed in Glory and Might is alive within me!

I declare a harvest of the seeds sown in tears,
over my family, over my journey, over my health, over my relationships,
spring forth now in righteous joy!

I declare this joy within me - a promised fruit of the Holy Spirit
cannot be replicated, stolen, or counterfeited!
For the Kingdom of God of which I am an heir
is not a matter of self and strife
but of righteousness, peace, and joy in the Holy Spirit.

I decree
the joy,
the delight,
the rejoicing
of the Lord, Yahweh
is my life-giving strength.

ROMANS 14:17, JOHN 15:11,
PSALM 16:11, NEHEMIAH 8:10,
ISAIAH 55:12, PSALM 30:5,
1 PETER 1:8

DECREE OF ADORATION

I declare You, O Lord,
Are worthy of all my
Affection,
All my praise,
All my worship.

I declare my heart overflows
With fountains of adoration
To the only King, Yahweh.

I declare the
Valor and the victory
Are Yours.

All greatness,
All glory,
All splendor,
All power,

I declare they are Yours!

I decree a release of adoration
Within my soul,
Like mighty rushing waters,
For Yours is the kingdom.
Yours is the power.
Yours is the glory.

Oh my soul, adore Him,
Lord Jehovah.

I declare you are authorized as the Head,
Exalted above all.

I declare you are sovereign,
Over all the sky and the earth.

I decree with my breath,
My heart,
And my soul
You, O Lord, You are great,
Mighty,
Majestic,
Magnificent,
Glorious, and sovereign over all creation!

1 CHRONICLES 29:11

DECREE OF STRENGTHENING IN THE LORD

I declare an infilling
of the resolve and the might
of the Lord, Yahweh.

Within my spirit
Within my soul
Within my body

I declare the strength
bursting forth in me roars from the
fierce majesty of His name,
and His throne.

I declare He fills me through His Spirit with
the Strength to stand - tender as a Shepherd!
the Strength to lead - sovereign as a King!

I declare
to the ones who have
surrounded me,
mocked me,
and come against me because of His name -
your arrogant attacks
will be shattered by My God,
the God of the Angel Armies!

As I stand for Righteousness, He protects me.
From His mighty throne in the Heavenlies, He thunders against evil!

I declare
He leads,
He rescues,
He protects,
and He gifts me eternal victory through
the blood of the Lamb and the word of my testimony!

I declare His strong right arm covers me
as He pours out His unmatched
strength upon me, His beloved and courageous one.

I speak to my inner man to
be strengthened by His Spirit
and to operate with power,
unlimited as the boundless glory
and wonder of His divine, all-powerful nature.

I declare within my birthright is the weapon of courage.
Courage like Daniel, to stand when all others bow.
Courage like Joshua, to trust when all others doubt.
Courage like Deborah, to rise up when all others cower.
I declare the words of David over my destiny:

"Be strong and courageous, and take action;
Do not fear nor be dismayed,
For the LORD God, my God, is with you. "

I declare
I am strong.
I stand firm.
My resolve comes from Him,
and Him alone.

EPHESIANS 3:16, MICAH 5:4, 1 CORINTHIANS 16:13,
JEREMIAH 16:19, ISAIAH 5:19, PSALM 140:7,
1 CHRONICLES 28:20, 1 SAMUEL 2:10, EPHESIANS 6:10

DECLARATION OF
TEARS TO BLESSINGS

I declare I am passing through
the Valley of Weeping,
My pools of tears turning to
springs of blessings.

PSALM 84:5-6

DECREE OF MY ALABASTAR JAR

I declare Jesus is King,
worthy of the finest gifts of my life,
worthy of the highest praises of my heart.

I declare a breaking of my alabaster jar,
releasing an outpouring of
the pure,
the genuine,
the costly praises of my heart
to soak the holy, beautiful feet of Yeshua.

I declare He is worthy, with the most valuable and precious oil of my life.

I declare He, alone, is worthy.

I declare He is the King, the Savior,
and I recognize Him - no matter the cost -
as the one and only Son of God.

I declare my children will know the aroma of anointed worship,
and the walls of my house for generations will be saturated with the
sweetest, mostly costly fragrance of love poured out unto Jesus.

JOHN 12:3

DECLARATION OF THY WORD

I decree Thy Word,
"It is written: 'Man shall not live on bread alone,
but on every word that comes from the mouth of God."

I declare Thy Word,
it is alive,
it is active,
it is sharper than any double-edged sword,
it is the divider of soul and spirit, joints and marrow,
it is the judge of thoughts and attitudes of the heart.

I declare Thy Word,
is a lamp for my feet,
is a light for my path,
is a shield for my refuge,
is a wise way for my life.

I declare Thy Word is flawless,
protecting and engulfing me in
the living breath of God:
teaching,
rebuking,
correcting,
and training me in righteousness!

I declare THY word equips me for every good work,
I declare the unfolding of Thy Word gives light,
I declare Thy Word has built my House,
for I heard the words,
and I believed the words of my Father:

my God, The Rock, my Savior,
who does not change,
who does not waiver,
who does not lie,
who delights in me!

I declare Thy Word,
the God-breathed scriptures,
are as important as the air I breathe!

Every word is Truth,
every word is Holy,
I break any agreement with the
world that has tried to
pervert, twist, and devalue Thy Word.
I declare Thy Word,
is power,
is flawless,
is life-giving,
and endures forever!

I decree an agreement with the words of Jesus:
"Blessed are those who hear
the word of God and obey it."

I declare I am obedient,
I declare I am blessed,
I love Him, I trust Him, and His Word.

Thy Word is the bread unto my destiny.

*ISAIAH 40:8, MATTHEW
24:35, HEBREWS 4:12, 2
TIMOTHY 3:16-17, PSALM
119:105, MATTHEW 4:4,
LUKE 11:28, PSALM 18:30,
PSALM 119:114, MATTHEW
7:24, PSALM 119:130*

DECREE OF THE WARRIOR

I declare our King is a mighty warrior
With eyes ablaze and head adorned with diadems.

The Crown of Royalty rests upon His head.

I declare the spirit of Victory rises within me.
I am not a victim but a victor!

I declare I am born of God:
The warrior spirit invigorating within me,
The spirit of peace flowing with me
I speak to my spirit and say:

Take heart! For my King has overcome the world!

I declare to every fiber in my body:
Be strong in Yahweh!
I release my flesh from the counterfeit victory of strife and toil
And declare victory comes only in the Lord and His mighty power.

I declare I have been given full authority by the King Himself
To trample on the serpents and the scorpions.
I have full power over
All the power of the Enemy,
And I declare no harm, no injury, no unjust acts will come upon me.

I declare His victorious conquest through the blood He shed on the cross
Is my legal basis to the spirit of the champion,
The victor and the warrior within me.

I declare victory rests with the Lord.
He stands beside me;
Before him my persecutors will stumble.
I declare they cannot defeat me.
My God is the Mountain Maker
Who sets them all in place.

I declare His power is irresistible, His Kingship is universal.

*REVELATION 19:12-16, JEREMIAH 20:11, LUKE 10:19, MARK 16:18, PROVERBS 21:31,
MALACHAI 4:3, DEUTERONOMY 20:4, 1 CORINTHIANS 10:13,
JOHN 16:33, EPHESIANS 6:13, EPHESIANS 6:10*

DECLARATION OF THE ROYAL PRIESTHOOD

I declare I am set apart by God and for God.

A chosen people,
a royal priesthood for the Kingdom,
a holy nation unto Yahweh,
God's special possession.

As a royal member of Kings, I declare
the wonderful deeds, virtues, and perfections of praise unto Him,
who summoned me by name out of darkness
and into His marvelous light.

I declare I walk in the luminosity of His excellence,
the radiating rays of His glory consume all darkness around me.

I declare I am precious in the sight of Yawheh,
no rejection of men,
slanders of this world,
or lies of Satan,
can remove the mantle the Royal Priest placed upon me.

Because my life lives in the one Living Stone,
who was rejected by men
but chosen, precious, and honored in God's sight,

I decree null and void are the works of darkness against me!

For I am a living stone,
being built into a wondrous spiritual house
to be a holy priesthood.

I declare the Spirit of God permanently dwells in me,
shaping my identity in truth and love -
guiding, directing, and sending me
as His Kingdom ambassador - His Royal Priest
to bring joy to the broken,
peace to the troubled,
hope to the lost.

Jesus, Yeshua, reign in the hearts of all mankind!

1 CORINTHIANS 3:16, 1 PETER 2:4-5, 1 PETER 2:9

DECLARATION
OF HIS BEAUTY

I declare He is beautiful, Jesus.
Beauty makes a home within His name, Yeshua.
His beauty bends my knee,
opens my hands,
overwhelms my spirit,
calms my soul,
straightens my spine,
yet brings me to total surrender.

I declare I live to pour out
the deepest wells of adoration,
for He is beautiful, for He is worthy.

I declare I live to behold the beauty of Jesus,
to gaze into the splendor of His face,
to stand in the endless blazing beauty of His Holiness,
to walk in humble obedience to His statutes.

I declare the fragrance of the beauty of Yeshua:
compassion that listens,
mercy that heals,
justice that is unshakable,
truth that never changes,
love that lays down,
and blood that shuts hell, death, and the grave!

I declare the fragrance of
Jesus, the Holy, beautiful one.
Savior! King! Friend! Messiah!

I declare a release of the living beauty of Jesus,
living waters in the deserts,
keys to the captives,
home to the prodigals,
light to the deepest, darkest valleys.

And I declare with the great crowd in Heaven:
'Hallelujah!
Praise the Lord!
Salvation and Glory!
Splendor and Majesty!
And Power, Dominion, and Authority belong to our God!'

I declare I worship Him, forever,
in Spirit and in Truth,
emptying myself of any and all glory,
my crown sitting at His feet,
cast with the twenty four elders, as we cry:

'Worthy are You, our Lord and God,
to receive glory and honor and power,
for You created all things;
by Your will they exist and came to be.'

I declare He is beautiful, unchanging, perfect in all ways,
and there will be a day when we will ALL declare:
'Hallelujah!
Praise the Lord,
for now the Lord our God,
the omnipotent, the Ruler of All,
Reigns!'

Holy.
Wonder.
Awe.
Beauty.
I declare I live to drench this world
in the righteous rains of beauty and freedom
that live in the only name,
Jesus.

REVELATION 4:10-11,
ACTS 2:28, REVELATION 19:1,
REVELATION 19:6, PSALM 29:2,
PSALM 27:4, PSALM 45:2,
SONG OF SONGS 5:10,
ISAIAH 33:17

DECLARATION OF THE
FIRE OF THE HOLY SPIRIT

I declare the wind,
the breath,
the Spirit of Holiness,
is kindling a fire deep within me,
a fire that cannot be quenched by the words or ways of this world!
A fire that does not bow in cowardice to cultural pressures,
or quiver in the face of the fear of man.

I declare it is a holy fire,
a baptism of fire,
cascading down from above,
from the One,
the mightiest One,
whose very sandals I am not worthy to untie.

I declare it is a holy, precious fire.
igniting within me a commitment
to feed the flame,
through prayer,
through the living Word,
through the praises of my lips!

I decree the fire of the Holy Spirit:
the bright, is now brighter,
the boldness, is now bolder,
the glory, is now more glorious.

For I have been baptized in fire and water into one body,
a Holy brotherhood,
through fire and flame,
drinking of one Spirit.

I decree a release of the fire of the Holy Spirit,
the burning up of all that is not of the Kingdom of Light,
in my life,
in my family,
and in the nations -
a wild burning fire of His Spirit
to move in power,
to move in authority,
to move in love,
to move in grace,
to move in truth.
For I am a child of the Most High,
a witness of Yeshua,
clothed in the fire of the Spirit of Holiness,
and destined to carry His name
unto the very borders of the Earth.

1 THESSALONIANS 5:19, ACTS 1:8, MATTHEW 3:11, LUKE 3:16,
ACTS 2:3, 1 CORINTHIANS 12;13,
EPHESIANS 4:30

DECLARATION OF
WORTHY IS THE LAMB

Jesus,
I declare Jesus,
He is infinitely worthy:
The one who opens the scroll,
The one who loosens the seal,
The worthy one!

I declare
All praise,
All glory,
All honor,
All wonder,
Upon Him.

The Lamb, the worthy one,
His feet that walked the earth for me,
His hands that were pierced for me,
His body that was beaten for me,
His blood that was poured out for me,
His spirit that was willingly given up for me,
His life that was resurrected for me!

I declare He is worthy to receive the full reward of His suffering
in my life,
in my family,
in His bride,
in every tribe,
in every tongue,
in every nation!

I declare I am zealous, burning with desire for good deeds,
May Jesus get his full reward!

I declare I desire to be sanctified, cleansed
and washed with the water of the Word,
May Jesus get his full reward!

I declare the church, His beautiful bride,
will walk in splendor, without spot or wrinkle,
holy and without blemish,
May Jesus get his full reward!

I declare Jesus, the sacrificial lamb,
bought me from the slave market of Satan,
redeemed me from death, hell, and the grave!
I declare He is worthy!
My liberator, my King, purchasing me
through His Body and His Blood
for eternity with Yahweh!

I declare my life is a life surrendered
unto the Lamb and committed to Him receiving His full reward:

I declare with the voices and choirs of angels,
numbering thousands upon thousands,
ten thousand times ten thousand,

"Worthy is the Lamb, who was slain,
to receive power
and wealth and wisdom
and strength and honor
and glory and praise!"

I declare there is no reward I desire
more than to see the Lamb receive the full reward of His suffering!

Worthy is the Lamb!

EPHESIANS 5:25-27, TITUS 2:14, REVELATION 5:9

DECLARATION JESUS IS LORD

I make a declaration with my mouth:

Jesus is Lord!
Jesus is Lord!

I declare every dark spirit trying to rob my King of His Lordship in my life - be gone!

I declare my life belongs to Jesus,
I believe with all my heart that the Father raised Him from the dead
And that all authority in Heaven and on Earth have been given to Him:

Jesus!

I declare He reigns supreme in my life,
The master and highest authority,
And I joyfully submit to His Lordship.

I declare there is only one Lord, Jesus Christ, by whom all things exist.
I align my heart with the words of the Father and declare:

Jesus, exalted high above all,
Jesus, the name above every name,
Jesus, the name at which every knee will bow
Jesus, the name which every tongue will confess is LORD,
To the glory of God the Father.

I declare a life committed to thrive under the
perfect, beautiful Lordship of Jesus.

I bring all areas of my life out of the shadows of darkness
and into the glorious light of His Lordship,
surrendering every counterfeit spirit of control and pride
to the gentle fires of the Master.
He is Lord of Lords and King of Kings - refining me in His holy fire.

All power, all authority, all control are His.

I declare that Jesus Christ is not only my Savior but He is my Lord,
He is the Lamb who has overcome, and I am with Him.

ROMANS 14:8, MATTHEW 28:18, ROMANS 10:9,
PHILIPPIANS 2:9-11, REVELATIONS 17:14, 1 CORINTHIANS 8:6